GARY JONES

New Orleans

Save Travels Ms. Graham! You will be missed.

— Shellie

First edition

This book was professionally typeset on Reedsy.
Find out more at reedsy.com

Contents

Introduction

In recent history, New Orleans has come to be known as the city that was heavily damaged by Hurricane Katrina in 2005. However, in a few short years, the Big Easy has managed to rise up again and restore itself to its former glory.

New Orleans was and still is one of the most fascinating cities in the world, and even Hurricane Katrina can't destroy the spirit of the locals.

The city is home to a unique melting pot of music, food, culture, voodoo, and the supernatural. Of course, you can't mention New Orleans without mentioning Mardi Gras or beignets.

Head on over to this vibrant American city that's historically- and culturally-rich. This guide offers you information on the city's history, the best times to visit the city, safety and weather, and transportation and going about in the city.

This informative guide lists some of the best and affordable hotels in the city. The guide also lists the best of everything from the city's restaurants, attractions, museums, art galleries, coffee shops, bars, and nightclubs. There's also a sample three-day itinerary that can serve as your guide whenever you come into the city.

1

Brief History and Background

During the 1690s, Robert de la Salle claimed Louisiana for the French. The French king during the time awarded the Company of the West a proprietorship, which enabled the company to develop the new colony.

The company's owner, John Law, appointed Jean-Baptiste Le Moyne de Bienville as the new colony's Commandant and Director General.

In 1718, Bienville realized his dream of the city of New Orleans. In 1721, engineer Adrian de Pauger laid out the city's streets. Many streets are named after Catholic saints and French royal houses. Bourbon Street, which many believed is named after the drink, is actually named after the Royal House of Bourbon.

THE CITY OF NEW ORLEANS.
AND THE MISSISSIPPI RIVER. LAKE PONTCHARTRAIN IN DISTANCE.

Spain. The French occupied New Orleans until 1763, when France sold the colony to Spain. The sub-tropical climate and two major fires destroyed many of the city's earlier structures. Early residents soon learned to build structures with brick and native cypress.

The Spanish colonists set up new building codes that required native brick walls and tiled roofs. When you walk along the French Quarter, you may eventually realize the architecture has more Spanish influences than French.

America. Through the Louisiana Purchase in 1803, the Americans began to occupy New Orleans. However, the Spanish and French Creoles saw the new occupants as 'low-class' and described them as uncultured people not suited to the Creoles' high society.

While the Creoles needed to engage in business with the Americans, the latter were never truly accepted. The Creoles then established Canal Street to keep the Americans from entering the old city. At Canal Street, you can see the old streetcars still rolling through.

The Haitians. An 18th century revolt in Haiti brought a number of immigrants and refugees to Louisiana. The Haitians were well-educated, were skilled artisans, and made their mark in business and politics.

James Pitot was one successful immigrant from Haiti who became incorporated New Orleans' first mayor.

People of Color. The Creole laws were more tolerant of slaves than that of the American laws. Under the Creole law, slaves can buy their freedom. Thus, New Orleans became a city with a lot of 'free people of color.'

Due to the mix of cultures and its geography, New Orleans is an eclectic city and is one of the country's most unique cities.

2

Best Time to Go to New Orleans and the Weather

The months of February to May are the best times to visit New Orleans. The weather is cool, and the streets are rife with celebrations. The popular Mardi Gras street parade runs for two weeks before the start of Lent.

If you want a quitter New Orleans, you can visit during December and January, when the city has a relaxed vibe. Around this time, you don't have to worry about reserving hotel rooms for about one year in advance.

If you want to save on hotel room rates, travel during the summer or fall. Know that the summer and autumn months are known for their humidity and heat, not to mention the hurricanes that are likely to pass through Louisiana.

February to May. These are the busiest months. If you want to join the festivities of the New Orleans Jazz & Heritage Festival or of the Mardi Gras, this is your best time to travel.

Note that hotel rates are high and hotel rooms may be scarce around this time. To ensure you get a room and to secure reasonable rates, book a few months or a year in advance.

A lot of the city's attractions are closed during Mardi Gras. Thus, if you want to see the attractions, travel at another time. Spring weather is pleasantly warm, with high temperatures averaging from the lower 70s to the mid-80s.

June to August. In contrast to the rest of the country where summers are the peak season, summertime in New Orleans is when tourists usually stay away. Tourists usually avoid the humidity and heat. Because of the low tourist traffic, expect to find cheap hotel deals.

The average high temperatures are in the low 90s, which can be uncomfortable for walking tours. Summers in New Orleans also tend to be rainy. So, bring a sturdy umbrella along with you.

September to November. The autumn months are usually a nice time to visit the city. Hotel rates are still cheap, and the temperatures range from the 80s (in September) and dip to the mid-70s (in November).

Be warned, late August and September are still part of the hurricane season. However, the better weather and the numerous fall season events make the city more enjoyable compared to visting during the summer.

December to January. Winter is also a good time to visit New Orleans. High temperatures are now in the 60s. This is perhaps one of most relaxing times to visit the city as spring festivals have not yet started.

Since winter has fewer tourists, you also get good deals on hotel rooms. If you like, swing by the city during the holidays when the city comes alive with holiday décor.

3

Safety in New Orleans

New Orleans is popular for foodies, history lovers, and party revelers. While the city is rich in entertainment and culture, your safety should be a main concern.

After Dark. If you're looking for a vibrant party scene, one of the best places to catch a party is at Bourbon Street, which is riddled with restaurants, music venues, and bars.

While Bourbon Street and the rest of the French Quarter are relatively safe during the day, nighttime can be a different story.

If you're not familiar with the city, stay in the more visible and safer neighborhoods. Districts outside the heart of the city may be less accommodating to visitors. Be sure not to get intoxicated if you're in these more unfamiliar parts.

Weather. New Orleans' proximity to the Gulf of Mexico makes it likely to be struck by hurricanes and tropical storms. Be aware of the weather forecast, especially during stormy weather.

Also be aware that weather forecasts are not always accurate. Listen to the residents (who rely on instinct) when they tell you to run to safety. During stormy weather, flooding is quite common.

Public Intoxication. Public urination, public intoxication, and similar offenses may put you in trouble. Thus, be on your best behavior when you visit the bars. Many visitors to the city may not be mindful of local laws and they may end up spending the night at the Orleans Parish Prison.

Driving. It can be challenge to drive in the city. From the airport, take a cab or other public transportation form. If you're bringing transport to the city, be aware of the parking signs.

The parking meters are marked clearly. If you illegally park, your vehicle is sure to get towed away. Secure a map before you go to New Orleans. Identify sparsely populated streets where you can park your car and get to be familiar with public parking spaces.

Road rage can be the norm in New Orleans driving. If you're at the receiving end of a road rage incident, stay in your car. Call the police and ask for help.

4

New Orleans Transportation

It can be tricky getting into New Orleans and getting around the city. Depending on your current location, you're either below sea level or at sea level. The Big Easy's streets are patterned on a Mississippi River bend, which also earns the city its 'Crescent City' moniker.

Aside from water, there are no other discernable landmarks to determine general direction. Water influences the way the locals describe their places: riverside (near the Mississippi River), lakeside (near Lake Pontchartrain), West Bank, and East Bank.

The East Bank is the Mississippi River's west side. To get to the other side, travel east across any of the bridges. If you're a first-time traveler to the city, transportation and the locations can be a bit confusing.

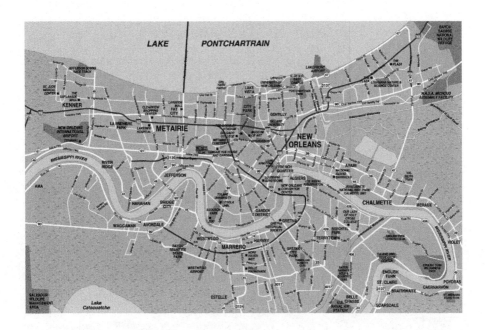

When it comes to transportation, you'll find that there are numerous options to help you navigate the Big Easy. Fear not. The city's expert drivers can help you get from Point A to Point B without you getting lost.

Airlines. Louis Armstrong New Orleans International Airport is located about 19km west of Downtown New Orleans. Taxis, shuttle buses, and public transport buses regularly traverse the French Quarter and downtown areas. The airport recommends that you arrive 2 hours before your flight departs.

Airport Shuttle. The New Orleans Airport shuttle can ferry you to any destination comfortably and safely with its fleet of gas-powered minibuses.

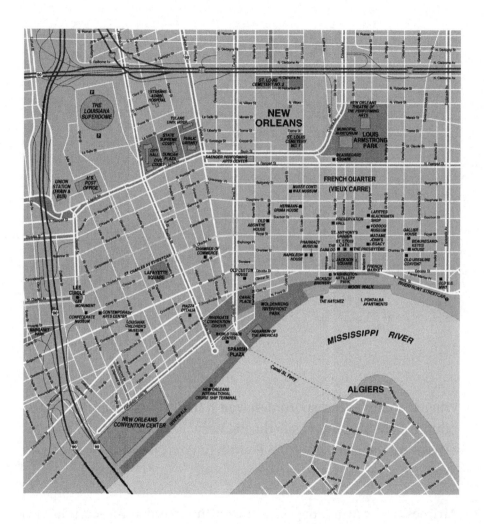

They transport passengers to Uptown and Downtown hotels, the French Quarter, Convention Center, and to Cruise Ship Terminals. The shuttle service welcomes large groups and vehicles that can accommodate handicapped individuals are available.

Lyft & Uber. If you want to travel through New Orleans comfortably, avail of ride sharing services like Uber or Lyft. With knowledgeable drivers who are mostly locals, you can learn more amazing stories about the Big Easy.

Rental Cars. You can rent cars in New Orleans when you want flexibility and freedom during your stay. You can choose from various car rental companies, with some of them located conveniently near or at the international airport.

Taxis. Taxis in New Orleans can be expensive. A city taxi ride can set you back $1.20 a mile, with an extra $1.00 charge for every extra passenger, and a $2.50 drop charge. West Bank trips cost an extra $2.00 to the meter.

Buses. The New Orleans RTA (Regional Transport Authority) provides public transport. However, transport between the New Orleans and Jefferson parishes involve separate transport agencies as the JET (Jefferson Transit) provides transport to Jefferson Parish.

Train Transportation. Three Amtrak trains terminate or pass through New Orleans. You can check online their fares and schedules. All Greyhound buses and trains depart and arrive from the Union Passenger Terminal located at 1001 Loyola Avenue.

Streetcars. The streetcar is one of the more charming and relaxing ways to get about the city. They can take you to destinations like shopping destinations, restaurants, and other attractions.

5

Top 5 Affordable Hotels

The most important thing to consider before going to New Orleans is securing your accommodation. If you don't have family or friends in the area with whom you can stay with, book a hotel of your choice as long as it's within your budget and if it's close to the area of your planned activities.

After all the dancing, dining, shopping, strolling , festival-going, and streetcar riding you're doing in the city, you need a comfortable place to stay. Whether you plan to book a hotel in the Garden District, French Quarter, some off-the-beaten-path place, or Downtown, the city's hotels always give you pleasant surprises.

If you're coming to the city for events or festivals, ask about special deals or packages. Certain hotels can set up transport from and to events and give discounts.

Below are five highly-rated and recommended budget accommodations that you can consider when you visit the Big Easy:

NOLA Jazz House

NOLA Jazz House, a hostel located on Canal Street, is decorated by local artists' unique paintings. The hostel is adjacent to the Canal at Clark Streetcar stop.

The hostel is an 8-minute drive away from the French Quarter and is 17.7km away from the Louis Armstrong New Orleans International Airport.
   It offers complimentary Wi-Fi, free breakfast, and evening drink socials. The hostel's accommodations include female dormitories, mixed dormitories, and private rooms.

Each simply furnished room features a fan, a desk, and a shared bathroom. The hostel also provides a shared kitchen with refrigerator and microwave oven.

You can borrow a guitar from the jazz house or you can bring your own. You can have a jam session with other guests at the spacious deck. You can also enjoy using free-of-charge desktops at the shared lounge.

Certain nights are reserved for group activities like martini nights and pub crawls. If you're bringing your own transportation, parking at the hostel is free.

The 1-star NOLA Jazz House is picked because of its proximity to the city's most important spots. It also received good reviews from previous guests.

Address: 3414 Canal Street
   Contact: (504) 975-1311

Wyndham Garden Baronne Plaza

Wyndham Garden Baronne Plaza, a hotel built in 1931, at the Historic Lower Business District, features the original Art Deco granite and stone façade. The hotel's lobby boasts of the original stained-glass skylights, columns, and marble floors.

The hotel is only one block away from the French Quarter and Canal Street. It's also highly accessible to some of the city's landmarks like the French Market, Riverwalk Outlet, Riverfront Streetcar Line, New Orleans Convention Center, the Mississippi River, the Super Dome, and the Aquarium of the Americas.

The hotel's rooms have a work desk, flat-screen TV, complimentary toiletries, and a seating area. Valet parking, a 24-hour front desk, complimentary Wi-Fi, and fitness center are also offered.

Every morning, PJ's Café serves fresh pastries and coffee. Business guests can make use of the business center, meeting facilities, and same-day dry cleaning. A tour and ticket desk is on hand to assist guests who want to explore the city.

The 3-star Wyndham Garden Baronne Plaza's location is favored by guests as the hotel is accessible to seafood restaurants, cafes, and city tours.

Address: 201 Baronne Street
  Contact: (504) 522-0083

Creole Gardens Guesthouse and Inn

Creole Gardens Guesthouse and Inn, a bread & breakfast at the Lower Garden District, features a banana tree-shaded courtyard. As with many accommodations in the city, complimentary Wi-Fi comes standard.

The inn is less than 10 minutes away from Ogden Museum of Southern Art and the National World War II Museum. The St. Charles Avenue Streetcar, which provides access to the French Quarter and the New Orleans city center, is one block away.

Each of the inn's accommodations has its en-suite bathroom and is decorated individually. Air-conditioning and cable TV are also available.
  Every morning, a complimentary breakfast (Southern-style) is served at the inn's main dining room. The bed & breakfast also welcomes pets.

The 3-star Creole Gardens Guesthouse and Inn is favored for its location. Guest also derive the best value for their stay at the inn.

Address: 1415 Prytania Street
  Contact: (504) 569-8700

The Whitney Hotel

The Whitney Hotel, which is located in Downtown New Orleans, is built on the site of a refurbished bank. In fact, the original vault doors are still there.

The hotel is less than a 10-minute drive away from the Mercedes Benz Superdome and Harrah's Casino. The hotel is also 1.1km away from the Ernest Memorial Convention Center. Additionally, it's a 15-minute walk from the vibrant French Quarter.

Each room comes standard with an ergonomic chair and work desk. You also get to enjoy complimentary bottled water as well. Each room's private bathroom has a hair dryer and toiletries. The rooms also come with a flat-screen TV with a device to enable video streaming.

Guests choose the 4-star Whitney Hotel for its location. The hotel is also favored for its proximity to cafes, seafood restaurants, and city trips.

Address: 610 Poydras Street
  Contact: (504) 581-4222

Omni Riverfront New Orleans

The Omni Riverfront New Orleans is located in the Arts/Warehouse District. You'd be delighted with the 7 restaurants that offer a wide variety of local and international cuisines.

Here, you can sample jumbo crab, Gulf fish, and other dishes in the modern dining area. You can enjoy drinks by outside tables.

The hotel is 3km away from both the Louisiana Superdome and the French Quarter. It's also 1.5km away from the heart of the city and it's located right next to the Ernest N. Morial Convention Center.

Cable TV with video games and pay movies are found in each richly-furnished accommodation. The rooms also have coffee- and tea-making facilities. Guests can also make use of the business center and 24-hour fitness. A launderette and concierge service are also available.

This 4-star hotel is famous because of its Arts/Warehouse District location, which has a string of dining places. The area is also a favorite of tourists who want to learn more of New Orleans' cultural heritage.

Address: 701 Convention Center Blvd
  Contact: (504) 524-8200

6

Best Famous Landmarks in the City

No other American city is more unique than New Orleans, which is known around the world for Cajun cuisine, jazz music, and Mardi Gras. The city is a cultural melting pot with a diversity reflected in aspects like food, music, architecture, and language.

When visiting New Orleans, explore the French Quarter, especially in the centrally-located Bourbon Street. Along the Mississippi River that borders the French Quarter are the docked Steamboat Natchez, tourists buying beignets, and horse-drawn carriages ready to show visitors around.

Apart from the French Quarter, the city has so many interesting areas to explore, from the glitzy Garden District to the Warehouse District.

As a walking city, New Orleans has various attractions in the vicinity of the French Quarter. However, if you want to venture into the Garden District, get on a street car. You can also take the bus, especially if you want to visit further areas like the zoo.

You cannot tour New Orleans in just one day. There are also so many attractions in the city, making it hard for you to decide which attractions to visit and which of them are considered the best.

Below are five well-known New Orleans landmarks and attractions that are worth a visit:

Presbytere

At the Presbytere, you can learn about the famous Mardi Gras tradition. The Presbytere, which is part of the Louisiana State Museum, has an interactive exhibit entitled 'Mardi Gras: It's Carnival Time in Louisiana' that features a collection of Mardi Gras memorabilia and artifacts.

The exhibit documents Mardi Gras' history, from its beginnings to the current traditions. You can also know more about Mardi Gras events in other areas of the state.

Louisiana State Museum

The building itself is an architectural wonder that you should visit. The Presbytere is constructed on the site of the presbytery (residence) of the Capuchin monks. The building was intended to aesthetically match the Cabildo on St. Louis Cathedral's other side.

From 1834 to 1911, the Presbytere was used as a courthouse – and as a commercial area previously – before it was acquired by the Louisiana State Museum.

Address: 751 Chartres St.
   Contact: (504) 568-6968
   Hours: Tuesdays to Sundays from 10:00am to 4:30pm and closed during Mondays and state holidays.

Audubon Aquarium of the Americas

The Audubon Aquarium of the Americas specializes in displays of both North and South America's aquatic life. Set by the French Quarter's edges and nestled on the Mississippi River's banks, the aquarium – one of the country's best-known aquariums – is managed by the Audubon Society.

On display are over 530 species that encompass over 10,000 animals. The exhibits are categorized by habitat. There's a Gulf of Mexico exhibit with a 40,000-gallon tank that showcases the region's sharks, turtles, and rays.
   The Amazon rainforest and river exhibit comes with a greenhouse, the Caribbean reef section has a walk-through glass tunnel, and the Mississippi River section features wildlife like paddlefish, catfish, and

NEW ORLEANS

the white alligator.

There's also the Great Maya Reef that can be experienced from a walk-through tunnel (30 feet) that's designed to look like a submerged Mayan city. Fish even swim among the ruins.

The eve-popular exhibits are the wildlife encounter programs, the penguins, and the sea otters. Optional extras are activities like snorkeling or scuba diving in the Great Maya Reef and getting up close with the African penguins.

Address: 1 Canal St.
    Contact: (504) 861-2537
    Hours: Tuesdays to Sundays from 10:00am to 5:00pm

Jackson Square and St. Louis Cathedral

Originally known as Place d'Armes, Jackson Square is the main square in the French Quarter's heart. The square's central portion is surrounded by greenery and trees and contains General Andrew Jackson's equestrian statue (1856).

St. Louis Cathedral

At the end of the square is St. Louis Cathedral. The cathedral's vicinity also is the location for two Louisiana State Museum buildings – the Cabildo and Presbytere. The park in front of the cathedral is a hangout for artists. The place is also frequented by tourists because of the area's restaurants and shops.

Jackson Square and the surrounding vicinity is laid out attractively along the Mississippi River's banks especially with the Moon Walk promenade, the Riverboat Docks, the Millhouse, and the various eclectic stores.

St. Louis Cathedral is one of Jackson Square's more prominent land-marks. The cathedral, which was built in 1794, is known for being one of the country's oldest continuous-use cathedrals. The cathedral was built on the location of two earlier churches. In 1987, Pope John Paul II visited the cathedral.

St. Louis Cathedral was built through Don Andres Almonester de Roxas' contributions. The Frenchman used part of his fortune to rebuild the city after the second great fire.

Jackson Square Address: 700 Decatur St.
   St. Louis Cathedral Address: 615 Pere Antoine Alley
   Jackson Square Hours: Wednesdays to Tuesdays from 8:00am to 7:00pm
   St. Louis Cathedral Contact: (504) 525-9585

French Quarter

If you're in New Orleans, make sure to thoroughly explore the French Quarter. You may even be booking an accommodation right at the French Quarter.

Set on a bend along the Mississippi River, the French Quarter – with its unique architectural style blend and vibrant atmosphere – is the Big Easy's most popular and most famous section.

French Quarter

The streets of the French Quarter (also called Vieux Carré) are lined with a mixture of lively Bourbon Street bars, a restaurant serving delicious food, historic monuments, and jazz clubs.

The old French Quarter buildings, some of which are over 300 years old, display French influences with wrought iron balconies, arcades, picturesque courtyards, and red-tiled roofs. A lot of these buildings now house restaurants, hotels, galleries, souvenir shops, and jazz spots.

Bourbon Street may look relatively calm by day, but it transforms into a boisterous and loud pedestrian area at night. During this time, you may want to look out for your safety.

Royal Street offers an eclectic mix of fine cuisine, history, and shopping opportunities with high-end stores, hotels, and galleries. One notable Royal Street structure is the Court of Two Sisters (built in 1832), which is now a restaurant that focuses on its jazz-themed brunch.

Since the French Quarter is pedestrian-friendly, you may want to wear comfy walking shoes. The French Quarter is also best experienced on foot. You may also want to go there riding streetcars, which run along Canal Street, the riverfront, and Rampart Street. Many city tours also go through the French Quarter.

French Quarter Sidewalk

The French Quarter is lovely throughout the year. In February, the French Quarter is usually busy as it is Mardi Gras. In April, the city holds its Jazz & Heritage Festival. New Orleans weather ranges from humid and hot to simply humid and mild. Summer months are usually the hottest. The comfortable and cool winter months may be punctuated with occasional downpours. Hurricane season is from June to November.

Garden District

A more charming side of New Orleans is the Garden District, which is an affluent residential area with mature trees, lovely mansions, and lush gardens. You can explore the area on foot and some companies even offer guided tours.

Camp Street, Prytania Street, and First Street are some of the best places to see the elegant, large 19th century mansions nestled among acres of land. While many visitors come to see the mansions, visitors may also find coffee shops and boutiques in the area.

Audubon Park is southwest of the Garden District. The park was established on the former location of the 1884 Industrial and Cotton Centennial Exposition. Within the park are oak trees, hothouses, the Audubon Zoo, Audubon Golf Club, a lot of green space, and numerous small lakes.

Garden District

The Garden District is a go-to place for first-time visitors and history buffs. Wear comfortable shoes as walking tours can last from two to three hours.

The most historic and easiest way to approach the Garden District is onboard the St. Charles streetcar, which also stops at the Audubon Zoo and the Tulane and Loyola Universities. You can also reach the Garden District through the Magazine Street bus or on foot.

What makes the Garden District even more fascinating is the fact that the area is home to many celebrities. You may even spot the homes of Sandra Bullock, John Goodman, father-and-son football legends Archie and Peyton Manning, and Anne Rice.

7

Best Museums

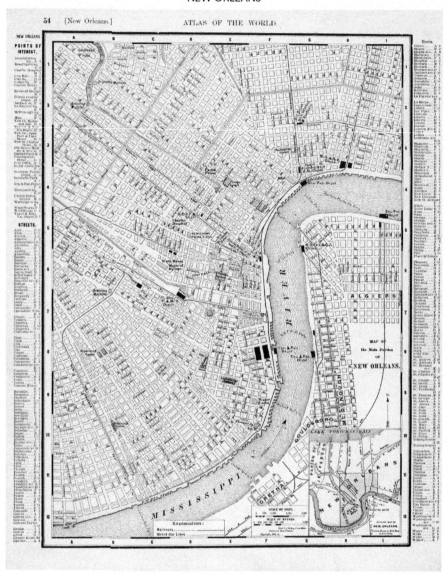

New Orleans Vintage Map

New Orleans is a city rich in history, as evidenced by the 45 plus museums that dot the city. Despite the vibrant history, people sometimes
forget to visit any museum as there's so much to do in the New Orleans.
You'll experience endless celebrations, festivals, and parties.

Locals and visitors are often enthralled by the activity on the streets, and they sometimes forget to slow down and reflect on the city's turbulent history.

When you're not partying, take time to visit any of the city's world-class museums, which are all located within a few miles of one another.

From admiring Southern fine art, to listening to jazz music while visiting a museum, to walking through a simulated Normandy exhibit and watching actual footage from World War II, you'd be pleasantly surprised to find out what these museums can offer you.

New Orleans has numerous historic homes and art collections that reflect its tumultuous past as well as French, Spanish, American, and African heritage. However, a sense of place also is crucial to the city's cultural landscape.

At the Ogden Museum of Southern Art, Southern artists take center-stage as they work on glass, oils, or pottery. At the Southern Museum of Food and Beverage in the Uptown/Garden District, you're taken to a world that highlights the cuisine of New Orleans and the American South.

The city's museums are not just about history. There are museums that highlight the city's current, contemporary culture. You can visit the arts corridors of St. Claude Avenue or Oretha Castle Haley. You can also visit the Contemporary Arts center, which features modern visual and performance art that exhibits New Orleans dance, music, and drag cabaret.

Take a break from the glitzy New Orleans nightlife and relax at five of the top museums in the city.

The National World War II Museum

The National World War II Museum, which is located at the Arts District/Convention Center neighborhood, is the entire country's official World War II museum. Here, you get to participate in first-hand simulations of some of the War's most significant battles.

You'll experience the battles that the United States participated in, from the prelude to war during the 1930s, to the Pacific Islands battles, to the Normandy Invasion.

The popular museum houses restoration works, exhibits, restaurants, and a period dinner theater. The museum, which was put up in 2000, honors the lives of the heroes who made sacrifices, so the current generation can enjoy freedom in peace.

Visitors can witness civilians' efforts and soldiers' combat experience. The National World War II Museum offers multimedia, unique exhibits, artifacts, and first-person narratives of wartime experiences.

The narratives cover how the War was won, how it began, and how it still impacts the world today. While touring the museum, you can view the collections of wartime aircrafts and bombers.

Address: 945 Magazine St.
   Contact: (504) 528-1944
   Hours: Mondays to Sundays from 9:00am to 5:00pm

New Orleans Jazz Museum

The New Orleans Jazz Museum at the French Quarter celebrates the type of music that originated in the city. Through multigenerational educational programming, dynamic interactive exhibits, engaging musical performances, and research facilities, jazz music is thoroughly explored.

Housed in the Old U.S. Mint building, the museum partners with national, international, and local institutions to promote the worldwide understanding of the music type as one of the most historically pivotal, innovative art forms in history.

The museum has collected, acquired, displayed, and archived artifacts that contribute to honor New Orleans' original music. The exhibits feature art from both musical and visual art by musicians and modern artists. The exhibits also feature musical instruments and recordings from some of the greatest jazz influencers and musicians.

You also get to see live performances from Tuesdays to Saturdays starting 2:00pm. The New Orleans Jazz Museum's website also streams online the performances to share with music and jazz enthusiasts from all over the world.

Address: 400 Esplanade Ave.
   Contact: (504) 568-6993, (800) 568-2566
   Hours: Tuesdays to Sundays from 10:00am to 4:30pm

New Orleans Historic Voodoo Museum

The New Orleans Historic Voodoo Museum is one of the city's most intriguing attractions. Nestled in the heart of the French Quarter, the affordable admission fees make the museum a go-to stop. Skeptics may even enjoy the museum's offerings.

The dimly-lit museum halls are lined with African artifacts used in voodoo practice, antique altars, and various works of art, letting visitors have a glimpse of an often-misunderstood and interesting aspect of the city's culture. The gift shop, aside from selling voodoo dolls, also has customized gris-gris like herbs, amulets, and potions used in spell casting.

Voodoo has been a vital part of the city's culture since the 1700s, when the city was established. Aside from the museum tours, visitors can join in the haunted cemetery tours through the downtown area.

The New Orleans Historic Voodoo Museum is an excellent place to visit with friends or family to know about the eclectic culture that makes New Orleans a unique American city.

Address: 724 Dumaine St.
Contact: (504) 680-0128
Hours: Sundays to Saturdays from 10:00am to 6:00pm, and open on most holidays.

New Orleans Museum of Art

The New Orleans Museum of Art, which is located in the Lakefront/Lakeview neighborhood boasts of an over 40,000-artifact collection spread throughout 46 gallery spaces. Some of the museum pieces even date back to 4,000 years.

The museum, which celebrated 100 years in 2011, features European sculpture and paintings from the 16th to 20th centuries, American and European drawings and prints, American sculpture, and paintings from the 18th to 19th centuries, American and European decorative arts, photography, and African, Asian, Pre-Columbian, Oceanic, and Native American art.

Some of the special collections housed in the museum include the Latin American Colonial Collection and the Peter Carl Faberge Treasures. Here, you can find works by Pablo Picasso, Braque, and Edgar Degas. The museum is also constantly evolving, which is why it's one of the South's top museums.

Aside from the art collections within the main building, you can also walk through the Sydney and Walda Besthoff Sculpture Garden. This sculpture garden is a 4-acre, 60-sculpture repository that features an amazing landscape of lagoons, foothills, Spanish moss, magnolias, pines, pedestrian bridges, and camellias.

The museum also hosts temporary exhibitions and had just held its first fashion-related exhibit entitled 'A Queen Within: Adorned Archetypes.'
    The New Orleans Museum of Art is committed to presenting and preserving its sculpture gardens and museum. It also aims to remain an institution that inspires, unites, and engages different cultures.

Address: 1 Collins Diboll Circle, City Park
    Contact: (504) 658-4100
    Hours: Tuesdays to Thursdays from 10:00am to 6:00pm, Fridays from 10:00am to 9:00pm, Saturdays from 10:00am to 5:00pm, Sundays from 11:00am to 5:00pm, and closed on Mondays.

New Orleans African American Museum

The New Orleans African American Museum, which is located in the historical Treme neighborhood, is dedicated to preserving, promoting, and protecting the art, communities, and history of the African diaspora and the African Americans in New Orleans during the Reconstruction, emancipation, and contemporary periods.

The museum is housed in the Treme Villa, which is one fine example of a city-based Creole villa. Constructed during the 1800s, the villa retains most of its original décor.

The Louisiana-Congo: The Bertrand Donation is one collection you should not miss. The collection features intricate African costumes, beadwork, textiles, masks, divination objects, and musical instruments.

Other New Orleans African American Museum tours explore Creole cottages, the St. Augustine church, Treme musicians and artists, and the gathering place of Congo Square.

Address: 1418 Governor Nicholls St.

Contact: (504) 566-1136

Hours: Tuesdays to Fridays from 1:00pm to 4:00pm, Sundays from 1:00pm to 4:00pm, and closed on Saturdays and Mondays.

8

Best Art Galleries

New Orleans is an art lover's haven. In fact, you can find art in almost every corner of the city. You'll find charming storefronts, courtyards, and warehouses filled with crafts, sculpture, and paintings.

Go inside one or more of these spaces to discover the history and local lore that shape this unique American city's character. Some of the interesting New Orleans streets where you can find quirky, traditional, and contemporary art include Julia Street, Royal Street, Magazine Street, and St. Claude.

Julia Street. Julia Street, which is also known locally as 'Gallery Row,' is home to renovated warehouses converted into classy art galleries with a contemporary, modern ambience. At every month's first Saturday at 6:00pm, you can enjoy wine and cheese tastings, music, and extended gallery hours at Julia Street.

Royal Street. Royal Street's mesmerizing courtyards draw you in with colorful canvases. You can also engage in conversation with a local artist at this street. Remember to drop by antique galleries like M.S. Rau, where you can see and acquire centuries-old artifacts from around the world.

Magazine Street. At the Garden District, you'd be delighted to explore Magazine Street's boutiques and get an antique or two. 'Art for Art's Sake,' one of the city's best art walks, occurs every autumn with gallery sales, free wine, and extended hours.

St. Claude. Set in the Bywater and Marigny neighborhoods, St. Claude features quaint local galleries. Each art gallery mixes into the vicinity's shops and music clubs, making St. Claude the perfect place to find hidden gems. Go to the 'Second Saturday Art Walk' from 6:00pm to 9:00pm and see the works of over 20 art vendors.

Spend a day or two at the city's beautiful art galleries. Below are five of New Orleans' best art galleries.

M.S. Rau Antiques

For over a century, M.S. Rau Antiques has been a beloved landmark in the French Quarter neighborhood. The 30,000-square-foot gallery boasts of astounding collections of jewelry, fine art, and 18th- and 19th-century antiques.

The gallery's mission has always been to provide customers with an unequalled antique-shopping experience. One reason is that the gallery's support personnel, research associates, and highly-trained sales staff are simply unparalleled.

M.S. Rau's collection is extensive and includes all categories of jewelry, art, and antiques. At the gallery, you're likely to find a Renoir painting, a Paul Revere sterling bowl, or a rare diamond.

If you're looking for a particular item and you can't find it at the gallery, M.S. Rau can find it for you. It has a worldwide network of contact and the gallery is certain to help you in finding exactly what you need for your collection.

Address: 630 Royal St.
   Contact: (504) 523-5660, (800) 544-9440

Arthur Roger Gallery

Located at the Warehouse/Arts District, Arthur Roger Gallery showcases art in various media. The gallery, which represents local artists as well as nationally-renowned artists, is one of the leaders of the local art scene.

Arthur Roger, in 1978, opened a gallery on Magazine Street. During the time, the New Orleans art scene was just blossoming, and the gallery soon attracted prominent visual artists like Ida Kohlmeyer and Robert Gordy.

In 1988, the gallery moved to its current location in downtown New Orleans. In 2004, the gallery opened another Arts District venue in the Renaissance Arts Hotel. Fortunately, Hurricane Katrina spared both of the gallery spaces. Arthur Roger Gallery continues to be active in New

Orleans' cultural revitalization.

Address: 432 Julia St.
  Contact: (504) 522-1999

New Orleans School of Glassworks & Printmaking Studio

If you want to have a unique art gallery experience, come to the New Orleans School of Glassworks & Printmaking Studio. Each day, the studio provides free demonstrations, enabling visitors to converse with artisans that specialize in glass-blowing, printmaking, torch-working, sugar-blowing, and metal sculpture letterpress.

As a visitor, you can design and make your own blown glasses, glass sculptures, and glass beads. The studio also offers demonstrations in copper enameling, metal sculpture, letterpress, printmaking, and bookbinding. The studio is an excellent idea for hands-on teambuilding, group receptions, and special events.

The New Orleans School of Glassworks & Printmaking Studio is three blocks away from the National World War II Museum. The studio's front room gallery displays designs created by visiting international and New Orleans craftsmen.

Address: 727 Magazine St.
  Contact: (504) 529-7279

Scene By Rhys Art Gallery

If you love music and want to appreciate New Orleans music better, there's a local art gallery that features art depicting the local music arena. Opened in November 2016, Scene by Rhys Art Gallery celebrates New Orleans music and musicians through a public display and artwork sales.

The brainchild of artist Emilie Rhys, the gallery honors musicians who benefit from the visual homage of them in a particular work. Musicians also benefit from the cash commissions brought to them from sales of artwork that feature them.

At the French Quarter gallery, you can flip through some sketchbooks that explore the New Orleans music world, as seen through the viewpoint of Ms. Rhys in the past six years.

Throughout Scene by Rhys Art Gallery, you will find originals by Ms. Rhys. Many drawings are sold without frames, yet they're supported by backing board that's acid-free.

Address: 708 Toulouse St.
   Contact: (504) 258-5842

Island of Salvation Botanica

Heighten your connection to the spiritual world at the Island of Salvation Botanica, which is located at the Faubourg Marigny/Bywater neighborhood. The gallery and store specializes in Voodoo medicinal herbs, religious supply, and local and Haitian artwork.

A trip to the gallery will enlighten and educate you on the rich blend of New Orleans' spiritual and cultural traditions. The gallery is a go-to place for locals for their religious supplies.

Sallie Ann Glassman, the gallery's owner, is an initiated Voodoo priest-ess and is recognized internationally for her art, readings, lectures, and healing ceremonies. You may want to have commissioned from Glassman a magical power talisman, a gris-gris bag, or a visionary painting.

You may even want to attend an authentic Voodoo ceremony at Achade Meadows, Sallie Ann's Voodoo temple. Sallie Ann and her group of initiated drummers, dancers, and singers perform the ceremonies.

Address: 2372 St Claude Ave., Suite 100
    Contact: (504) 948-9961

9

Top 5 Restaurants

New Orleans is known for its beignets, gumbo, jambalaya, and Cajun and Creole cuisine, and restaurants serving such cuisine are dotted all over the city. It's really hard to determine which city restaurants are the best, considering each of them offers sumptuous local, international, and fusion food.

Below are five of the city's best places to grab a bite.

Piece of Meat Butcher Shop and Restaurant

Piece of Meat Butcher Shop and Restaurant respects time-honored cooking traditions. The restaurant's tight menu has something to offer everyone – from sandwiches with funny names to French terrines to vegan sandwiches.

The restaurant's owners/butchers also put their stuff out in the open. Diners can eat sandwiches at a counter surrounding the working butchers.
   The Piece of Meat Butcher Shop and Restaurant's butchers work out of a tiled space that feels like they have been serving the community's meat requirements for a long time.

Address: 3301 Bienville Street
   Contact: (504) 372-2289

Barrows Catfish Restaurant

Barrows Catfish Restaurant opened in 1943. It is known its catfish platter offerings. The restaurant suffered heavily from Hurricane Katrina and had to close down.

The restaurant has now reopened in a new location, and people can get to order their old favorites. Here, you can enjoy fried, thick-cut catfish and a potato salad side and served with buttered sandwich bread.

Address: 8300 Earhart Blvd #103
   Contact: (504) 265-8995

Longway Tavern

The stylish Longway Tavern is housed in a 1794 building. It serves as a reminder to the people of New Orleans that the French Quarter is and will always be a tight-knit neighborhood.

The everyday bar serves smart cocktails and artfully-arranged pub food like salmon confit with yogurt and cucumber, Caesar salad topped with fried and crispy chicken skin, and radish with caviar and goat butter.
   Longway Tavern also has a charming brick courtyard. All the food is prepared in small plates to encourage the community tradition of sharing.

Address: 719 Toulouse Street
   Contact: (504) 962-9696

Auction House Market

Auction House Market is characterized by its stark white walls, rust-colored velvet stools, soaring ceilings, and gold accents. This elegant food stall is located in a defunct warehouse. The food market is currently a glitzy destination for sushi, casual cocktails, healthy food, and Indian & Mediterranean cuisine.

Address: 801 Magazine Street
  Contact: (504) 372-4321

Pythian Market

Pythian Market is one of the city's latest food halls. Here, you get to enjoy barbecue, mac and cheese balls, poké, Jamaican jerk chicken, and fried oysters. While the business is fairly new, it's housed in one of the city's more historic buildings.

With an area of 11,000 square feet, Pythian Market is located in a 1908 building that was once used by Grand Lodge Colored Knights of Pythias – a black fraternal organization. Once called the Pythian Temple, it had a rooftop garden, a theater, a local NAACP office, and various black-owned businesses.

The building was used as boat builder Higgins Industries' offices in World War II. By the 1950s, the building was known as the Civic Center Building. The building was abandoned after Hurricane Katrina. Nowadays, the Pythian Market is a popular hangout for cocktails as well as a variety of food options.

Address: 2002, 234 Loyola Ave
  Contact: (504) 481-9599

10

Best Coffee Shops

While New Orleans has a long, coffee culture history, it's just relatively recently that the coffee roasts, styles, and techniques have diversified fully. The coffee shop scene in the city has grown from plain brewed coffee to the proliferation of coffee shops with relaxing and entertaining atmospheres.

At such places, you can get a cortado, pour-over, or an Oji-brewed, one-bean cup of coffee. While you can still enjoy café au lait and chicory, you now have many coffee options to choose from.

The list of the city's best coffee shops offer the most unique coffee offerings within elegant interiors.

Cherry Espresso Bar

Located in the city's Uptown district, Cherry Espresso Bar is the brainchild of barista Lauren Fink. She uses coffee from micro roasters like Quills Coffee, Heart Roasters, Roseline Coffee, and Ruby.

Cherry Espresso Bar also offers public cuppings twice monthly where the café staff orient customers through tasting coffee's sensory experience.

Address: 1649, 4877 Laurel Street
   Contact: (504) 875-3699

Rouler

Rouler, which is located at the Central Business District, is for the serious cycling enthusiast who also loves a serious cup of coffee. From its previous Canal Street location, the café still offers bike repair services, riding apparel, and a mean cup of chai latte.

Aside from coffee, Rouler also offers a lunch and breakfast menu, making the café a one-stop shop for the cyclist who needs to build up his energy reserves.

Address: 601 Baronne St C1
  Contact: (504) 327-7655

French Truck Café

The yellow truck on Magazine Street has now become the little yellow café called French Truck Coffee. Aside from coffee of all varieties, the coffee shop serves breakfast, beer, lunch, wine, and light evening meals.

French Truck Café directly gets its beans from farmers. This means the staff may occasionally take off for coffee regions like Costa Rica and other places. The café's coffee beans are also sold all over the city in restaurants, other coffee shops, and grocery stores.

If you want to get the most out of the café's products, it's best to enjoy your coffee at the actual French Truck Café on Magazine Street.

Address: 1200 Magazine Street
  Contact: (504) 298-1115

Drip Affogato

Drip Affogato, which is located at the Warehouse District, features a combination of ice cream and coffee products. The shop features French Truck coffee and Creole Creamery ice cream to create all kinds of sweet-bitter, cold-hot concoctions.

Go for the Cookie Monster with Mexican hot chocolate ice cream, hot chocolate, and cookie crumbles. You can also try the Classique with pistachios and Tahitian vanilla ice cream, or stroopwafel with espresso.

While you can get plain ice cream or coffee at Drip Affogato, why settle for simplicity when you can get all the ice cream works?

Address: 703 Carondelet Street
   Contact: (504) 313-1611

Congregation Coffee

Congregation Coffee, which is a micro roaster, serves coffee made from responsibly-grown and locally-roasted coffee beans. Located at Algiers Point/West Bank, you can get a delicious freshly-made cappuccino.

You can pair that cappuccino with Levee Baking Company's pastries or Windowsill's baked pies.

Address: 240 Pelican Ave
   Contact: (504) 265-0194

11

Top 5 Bars

Not only is New Orleans known for its Mardi Gras celebrations and beignets, it's also known for its cocktails. Whether you're at a contemporary mixology spot, a neighborhood pub, or a high-end hotel bar, you're likely to find friendly, skilled bar staff who are ready to mix you a refreshing cocktail glass.

Try a Sazerac (a rye whiskey), a Ramos Gin Fizz, or a Brandy Milk Punch. You can also sample local beers and international wines too. No matter what you're enjoying, the essence of a bar is that you get to enjoy a good drink in good company. Below are five of the best bars at the Big Easy.

The Sazerac Bar

The Sazerac Bar has been concocting drinks for locals since 1914. An Old World charm prevails at the 1800s building the bar's located in. Here, you'll find a traditional wood bar, tiled floors, and dozens of paintings and portraits of Napoleonic battle scenes and of Napoleon.

At the Sazerac Bar, you can also listen to Eroiqua, which Beethoven composed for Napoleon and is playing often on loop. While the bar draws in a lot of tourists, New Orleans locals also regularly go to the spot. Most of them are French Quarter professionals having a post-work cocktail or are having lunch meetings.

Address: 130 Roosevelt Way
   Contact: (504) 648-1200

The Carousel Bar & Lounge

What makes the Carousel Bar & Lounge iconic is that it's the only revolving bar in the city. The century-old bar has a fully-illuminated centerpiece that consists of a red and gold 25-seat merry-go-round with a 360° bar set in the middle of it.

The centerpiece makes people want to go into this bar, especially on a quiet afternoon without the weekend and evening crowds. The cultural and historical aspects of the Carousel Bar & Lounge heighten the cocktail drinking experience. The drinks program is also something that's noteworthy.

Address: 214 Royal Street
  Contact: (504) 523-3341

Seaworthy

Seaworthy, an oyster and cocktail bar, is set within the Ace Hotel. The bar's name is worthy of its maritime theme, and one could imagine a host of loud seamen occupying the bar comfortably.

Dark wood and Prussian blue frame the shucking area and oyster baskets and sea life scenes decorate the walls. The Gulf Coast oyster selection seamlessly works with the different drinks.

The oysters' brine flavor cuts through the cocktails' sugar and citrus, letting you drink in the many aspects of the sea life in Louisiana.

Address: 630 Carondelet Street
  Contact: (504) 930-3071

Hot Tin

At the rooftop of the remodeled Pontchartrain Hotel is the bustling Hot Tin bar. On the way leading to the bar, you're treated to a flurry of conversation, décor that features wonderful and weird artifacts, and posters.

Hot Tin's main room is like a post-war, colonial loft, decorated with vintage typewriters, sepia photographs, and old postcards and letters. The cocktail menu features conventional drinks but are named uniquely. Gin and rum cocktails at the Hot Tin are given names like The Seersucker or The Skyliner.

Address: 2031 St Charles Avenue
   Contact: (504) 323-1500

Barrel Proof

Lower Garden District neighborhood residents frequent Barrel Proof, a bar that's dedicated to whiskey and all things whiskey. In this windowless, low-ceilinged bar, you are treated to a selection of 300 bourbons, whiskies, scotches, and ryes.

You can come here all the time, and you never tire of this place. Cocktail and alcoholic selections range from the usual bar room fare to Japanese imports. At Barrel Proof, if you're not sure about ordering whiskey, there are other alternatives as well.

Address: 1201 Magazine Street
   Contact: (504) 299-1888

12

Top 5 Night Clubs

New Orleans is charmingly vibrant by day, yet it becomes rowdier by night. By this time, all the cocktails flow and the dance music turns up. The Big Easy, especially at Bourbon Street, literally becomes one massive dance floor and music club.

New Orleans has all its nightclub bases covered, from jazz music, to house music, or even Latin dance music. Many of these nightclubs are concentrated in Bourbon Street and Frenchmen Street, which are all accessible from most hotels in the city.

There are many nightclubs that you can go to. Here are some of the best places where you can start.

The Metropolitan Nightclub

The Metropolitan Nightclub, which is located in the Warehouse District, is considered the city's premier video DJ dance club. The smoke machines and intricate lighting get you in the mood, and the bass beat goes on and on.

Music in the club includes hip hop, Top 40, rock, mash ups, and pop in one part of the club. Another room plays techno, house, and dub and breaks. The walls are littered with flat-screen TVs so people can easily dance to the tune of the DJ's music.

Valet parking and table service are available. While you may find it tedious to get a drink in most clubs in the, you'd be delighted that you can easily find a bar station at the Metropolitan Nightclub.

Address: 310 Andrew Higgins Blvd
Contact: (504) 568-1702

Bourbon Heat

Bourbon Heat is best known for its courtyard setting and happy hour offerings. The club is located on the upper floor. At the club, you'll find all kinds of partygoers moving rhythmically on the dance floor.

As soon as you step into the club, you'll get excited when you hear the thumping music from either video or live DJs. The smoke billows and the lights shine as patrons dance the night away to new and old favorites.

If you want to take a break from the Bourbon Heat action, head out to the balcony. Take a look at the Bourbon Street pedestrian and vehicle traffic and take a breath before heading back in.

Address: 711 Bourbon Street
  Contact: (504) 324-4669

Cat's Meow

Located at Bourbon Street, the famous Cat's Meow is known for great karaoke and its happy hour specials. There's a rumor that Bill Gates and the Smashing Pumpkins have sung some great tunes here.

The action goes on all night and the nightclub is packed until the early hours of the following day. Whether you want to dance on the floor or sing center stage, there's always a fun activity for you at Cat's Meow.

Address: 701 Bourbon Street
  Contact: (504) 523-2788

Blue Nile

If you want to experience real nightlife at the Big Easy, go to Blue Nile at Frenchmen Street. The club is housed in one of the street's oldest structures, which was built in 1832. Blue Nile always brings in some of the best national and local traveling musical acts. The full bar also never disappoints its patrons.

The gold and blue interior gives off a relaxed vibe, making the transition from business to leisure quite simple. Blue Nile features two-floor entertainment, including an upper-floor balcony that overlooks Frenchmen Street.

Address: 532 Frenchmen Street
  Contact: (504) 948-2583

Republic New Orleans

Republic New Orleans, which is located at the Warehouse District, is housed in a former warehouse that dates back to 1852. The massive historic space is divided into three clubs – the ground-level main dance club, the mezzanine on the upper floor, and the Green Room that's an excellent place to hold a private event.

Massive chandeliers are suspended from the ceiling of the space, and partygoers dance the night away to live music and DJs. Republic New Orleans has bars on each side of the floor to keep customers happy. You'll be seeing a younger crowd here, so be prepared to feel some energy on the dance floor.

Address: 828 S Peters Street
Contact: (504) 528-8282

13

List of Unique Things you can do Only in New Orleans

The Big Easy is not your average American city. Mixed together with the modern skyscrapers are evidence of the city's storied colonial past.

Even the current traditions and cuisine still reflect the vibrant culture of its past occupants.

Because of this, the city of New Orleans is a must-see. The National World War II Museum attracts hundreds of thousands of visitors annually. The New Orleans Museum of Art boasts of an impressive collection of international, national, and Southern art.

New Orleans is not just about its tree-lined promenades and museums. There's so much more to discover. Go to the quieter attractions like the City Park. You may even go on a local swamp tour to explore the vicinity's natural treasures.

The Big Easy is one of the country's most unique and dynamic cities. In here, you get to do activities and see things that you can't find in other countries. Below are some activities that you can do only in New Orleans.

Mardi Gras

Mardi Gras. Many people come to New Orleans to celebrate Mardi Gras, which is the main event of the city. Celebrations last for two weeks and end on Shrove Tuesday, which is the day before Ash Wednesday.

Celebrations include parades that occur almost daily. The festivities and entertainment intensify as Mardi Gras draws to a close. Onlookers crowd the sidewalks and balconies to see the parades and catch beaded necklaces tossed up from decorated floats.

While the entire French Quarter is packed with revelers, Bourbon Street has the highest concentration of activities and crowds. French settlers introduced the tradition to the city. By the end of the 19th century, the two-week Mardi Gras tradition became popular.

City Park. City Park encompasses over 1,300 acres and houses a number of attractions that include the New Orleans Museum of Art and Sculpture Garden and the New Orleans Botanical Garden.

Of interest to families and children are Storyland, the Carousel Gardens Amusement Park, and the City Splash water park. City Park is also home to walking paths, an 18-hole golf course, and tennis courts.

City Park also lays claim to have one of the world's largest collection of live mature oak trees, with one tree that's almost 800 years old.

Steamboat Natchez. When you board the paddle steamer Steamboat Natchez, you get a different view of the Mississippi River and the city of New Orleans as well.

Steamboat Natchez

The two-hour harbor cruises provide narration on certain sites with an optional Creole cuisine lunch. The dinner cruise features a buffet-style dinner, a live jazz band, and sweeping views of the city.

There are also special cruises for occasions like Valentine's Day, Easter, Christmas, Mother's Day, and other holidays. If you want to board the Steamboat Natchez during the peak season, book your tour in advance.

Audubon Zoo. Located at 6500 Magazine Street, the Audubon Zoo boasts of a selection of exotic and domestic animals amid lush grounds.

While the zoo is 12km away from the centrally-located French Quarter, there are still so many reasons to visit this nature reserve.

Some of the zoo's residents include jaguars, giraffes, orangutans, leopards, rhinos, elephants, alligators (including the white alligator), and lemurs. During summer, The Audubon Zoo offers visitors the opportunity to cool off in the Cool Zoo, which is a splash park.

Music Box Village. Located at Rampart Street, Music Box Village resembles a wooden forest that's part music venue and part acoustic playground. Tiny 'houses' made of metal, plastic, and wood contain their own musical 'instruments.' These are wind, percussion, or electronic devices hooked into floors and windows.

Kids would surely love to explore Music Box Village. You and your family can have fun while running around, exploring, and making a lot of noise. When local bands come, they are to use the 'instruments' themselves.

Ghost and Cemetery Tours. Ghost tours at the French Quarter are highly popular among visitors. Operating on the payment models of 'pay what you can' or 'pay what you like,' the ghost tours happen twice a night at 7:30pm to 8:15pm.

During the French Quarter ghost tour, you'll see notable haunted locations like Hotel Monteleone and Pirate Alley. Topics discussed in the tours include modern true crime stories, yellow fever, and some of haunted tales set in New Orleans.

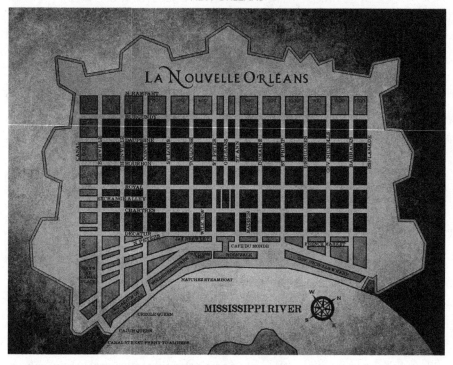

Cemetery tours are also 'must-experience' activities when you visit New Orleans. Many tours start at the rear of a Rampart Street bar. When you visit the tombs, keep an eye out for the tomb of Marie Lauveau, New Orleans' legendary voodoo queen.

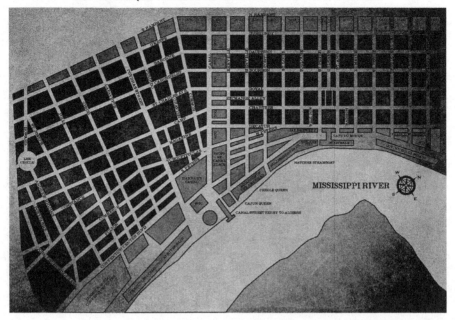

While you don't necessarily feel that a ghost can haunt you at the cemetery, a trip to the cemetery is still worth it as you get to admire the magnificent stonework on many of the tombs.

Treme Fall Fest. The Treme Fall Fest falls every first week of October, with the St. Augustine Catholic Church hosting the event. During the festival, local artists and businesses provide delicious food and free musical performances. There are also children's activities like building projects and painting.

Jackson Square

Some of the artists that had participated in past events included Shannon Powell, Kermit Ruffins, Leroy Jones, and John Boutte, among others.

The Treme Fall Fest, which is a donation-based event, was initiated to raise money for the church. The fest is held on the church's surrounding streets, located at the corner of Gov. Nicholls and Henriette Delille Streets.

National Gumbo Day. National Gumbo day is observed annually every October 12, and many locals would say New Orleans is the only place to eat an excellent gumbo. That's the reason why this dish deserves its own special celebration.

This Cajun dish includes chicken, shellfish, shrimp, and sausage along with spices and vegetables like tomatoes and okra. If one of your vacation days is on October 12, be sure to check out some of the best gumbo places like Galatoire's, Herbsaint, Royal House, and K-Paul's Louisiana Kitchen.

Other restaurants serving good gumbo include Dooky Chase's Restaurant, La Provence, Cochon Butcher, The Praline Connection, and Jaeger's Seafood Restaurant.

Sample the Beignets. No trip to New Orleans is complete without you sampling the city's most famous dessert, the beignet. Most visitors to the city normally would have their beignet fix at Café du Monde at the French Quarter. However, there are a number of cafés in the city where you can indulge in these sweet treats in savory and sweet variations.

Beignets, which is French for 'bump,' are deep-fried pastries served hot and sprinkled with powdered sugar. Beignets and Mardi Gras are what make New Orleans the vibrant city that it is.

Beignets

Magazine Street. With a six-mile stretch from Canal Street by the Mississippi River to Audubon Park, Magazine Street traverses from the Central Business District to the Arts/Warehouse District and through Uptown and the Garden District.

Named originally for a warehouse that Governor Miro built to contain exports like Kennedy tobacco, Magazine Street's stores offer a delightful contrast to the conventional shopping mall experience. Shop clusters integrate seamlessly with charming residences.

Moreover, you can find shops and renovated warehouses selling pottery, houseware, clothing, period furniture, books, clothing, toys, glass, soaps, jewelry, and china.

At Magazine Street, you can also enjoy a leisurely walk and you'll surely come upon a restaurant or coffee shop where you can relax after a busy walking day. The bus that goes to Magazine Street departs from Canal Street.

French Quarter Shopping. If you want to take home the most unique finds, you're most certain to find them at the French Quarter. Here, you get a unique shopping experience with timeless elegance and among majestic architecture.

At the French Quarter, which is also a National Historic Landmark, you can browse through a mix of shops from voodoo dolls to haute couture. You'll also find local art, jewelry, antiques, and all kinds of fleur-de-lis stuff.

Crescent City Blues & BBQ Festival. There are so many things that New Orleanians are good at, and one of them is to throw a grand party! One festival that's held during October is the Crescent City Blues & BBQ Festival.

Held annually, the festival features notable acts including Samantha Fish, Walter 'Wolfman' Washington, and Jimmie Vaughan, among others. Aside from the blues fest, expect to enjoy a lot of local food as well as barbecue.

The 2018 edition of the Crescent City Blues & BBQ Festival is at Lafayette Square Park and runs from October 12, 2018 to October 14, 2018. If you can't attend or you miss this festival, the city has a lot of live music offerings. If you miss the barbecue, go on a New Orleans food tour.

Halloween in New Orleans. If the weather is not an issue to you, one of the best times to visit New Orleans is during Halloween. Some of the Halloween activities to enjoy in the city include the Voodoo Festival, Halloween Carnival, Voodoo Tour, and Boo at the Zoo.

The Voodoo Festival is a yearly event that brings internationally-known musical artists to City Park during the pre-Halloween weekend. For 2018, visiting artists include Mumford & Sons, Childish Gambino, A Perfect Circle, Modest Mouse, Third Eye Blind, Marilyn Manson, and many more.

The Halloween Carnival takes place during the weekend before Halloween.

The Voodoo Tour allows you to learn more about this misunderstood practice. If you want to know more about voodoo, this is an enjoyable and affordable opportunity to do that. For the voodoo tour, you get to 'pay what you wish.'

Boo at the Zoo is a family-oriented Halloween event. At the Audubon Zoo, take your kids to trick or treat. Enjoy and be scared at a ghost train and a haunted house. Join in entertainment and play other games as well.

14

3-Day Travel Itinerary

New Orleans is all about indulgence, the supernatural, and fabulous food, shopping, and nightlife. While 3 days of touring the city may seem short, you can see the city in a nutshell and you get to discover what makes the Big Easy tick.

In three days, you can see the city's best attractions, learn history through its museums, eat beignets and gumbo, and dabble in the supernatural and occult by visiting the old graveyards and catching a glimpse of Madame Delphine LaLaurie's house.

This 3-day travel itinerary is just a sample of what you can do in the Big Easy. The sample travel itinerary is great for first-timers and it gives them a view of how New Orleanians live.

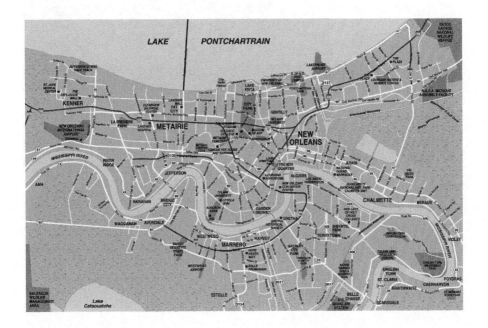

Day 1

Jackson Square. You don't spend a lot of time at Jackson Square, and the things that make it remarkable are the activities you can enjoy between

97

St. Louis Cathedral and Jackson Square.

In the area, you get to see and enjoy the street performers like jugglers and jazz musicians. You also get to see individuals wanting to dabble in voodoo. Jackson Square is exciting and lively, and it's an excellent starting point for your New Orleans tour.

The French Quarter. At the French Quarter, you get to see bustling street activity, majestic architecture, and a lot of bars, restaurants, and candy shops. Here, you can enjoy taking pictures, going inside bookstores, people-watching, and indulging in delicious sweet and savory treats.

If you want to know more about the French Quarter, it is best that you join a walking tour.

The French Market and Decatur Street. The French Quarter is the location of Decatur Street, where you can find a host of the city's most popular restaurants.

There are also tour companies, souvenir shops, and donkey-drawn carriages. Go to the French Market that is parallel to Decatur Street and shop for souvenirs.

Café du Monde. This café, which specializes in beignets, is just across Jackson Square. The café serves drinks and beignets, and the items on the menu are reasonably priced. Because the prices are affordable, you may be tempted to come here multiple times while you're in New

Orleans.

Café du Monde

Frenchmen Street or Bourbon Street Nightlife. The first day only covers a relatively small area of the city. Thus, you may still have the time to end the day by hitting the clubs and bars at Bourbon Street or Frenchmen Street. Frenchmen Street is best known for jazz music, while the noisier Bourbon Street is known for debauchery and raucous partying.

Day 2

Plantation Visit. New Orleans is actually a large city, and the French Quarter and its surroundings only comprise a sizeable minority of the city's area.

Begin your day by going on a plantation tour, and reflect on the sad histories of slavery. However, not many plantation museums are upfront on the gruesome details, and they just merely focus on the genteel plantation life.

Oak Alley Plantation

One of the best plantations to visit is **Oak Alley Plantation**, which does a great job of tackling both the horrible and glamorous aspects of plantation life including documents, stories, and exhibits of the lives of the wealthy owners and their slaves.

Phone (225) 265-2151 (Oak Alley)

Other plantations worth a visit include the Houmas House Plantation, the Laura Plantation, the Whitney Plantation, and the Nottoway Plantation.

The Bayou. While you can know the basic aspects of New Orleans life through touring the city, you can also get to know other activities locals enjoy outside the city. One of these activities is going to the bayou.

Coastal New Orleans and many parts of Louisiana are home to wetlands, or the bayou. Here, you can see interesting wildlife, cypress swamps, and a delicate ecosystem.

Explore the bayou on an airboat. You can even hold baby alligators at a local rescue center.

Day 3

The Garden District. The Garden District is home to the city's elite. While most swanky residential areas are exclusive only to residents, the Garden District actually welcomes tourists and locals to ply the streets.

You can search for the houses used in American Horror Story or you can catch a glimpse of celebrity homes. At the Garden District, you not only get to admire beautiful architecture, you also get to relax a bit when you see the tree-lined streets.

Lafayette Cemetery No. 1. Within the Garden District is the Lafayette Cemetery, which has inspired author Anne Rice to work on her vampire novels that feature Lestat.

The cemetery is also a must-see as it's one of the few cemeteries in the country with above-ground tombs. While you can explore the tombs on your own, there's also an added advantage if you join the cemetery tours.

Magazine Street. Want to buy some eclectic and garish finds? Go to Magazine Street. It's also a great place to grab a decent meal. It's also where you can see Mardi Gras costumes, antiques, and unique souvenirs.

Ghost Tour Evening. There's never a shortage of ghost stories in New Orleans. If you do love a horror story, take the last tour of the night. The crowds are a bit older and the stories are scarier.

It's also amazing that you can bring your alcoholic drinks on the tour. If you ever feel a bit scared, you can just have a sip and momentarily forget your fear of the dark.

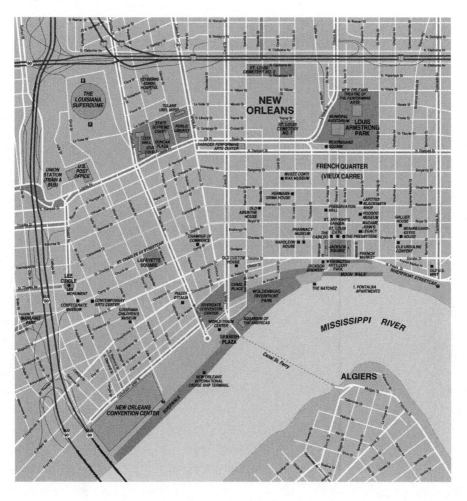

15

Conclusion

When you're in New Orleans, you're transported to a charm that you can never experience anywhere else. When in New Orleans, absorb the music of blues and jazz, indulge in Cajun cuisine, and revel in the parades and colors of Mardi Gras.

If you seek a great time, there's no better place to go than New Orleans.
   Whatever your destination in the city is, you'll always find something to delight in – be it New Orleans' Mardi Gras celebrations, music, architecture, food, or the vibrant nightlife.

Have a Great Trip !

Thank You

I want to thank you for reading this book! I sincerely hope that you received value from it!

If you received value from this book, I want to ask you for a favour .Would you be kind enough to leave a review for this book on Amazon?

This document is geared towards providing exact and reliable information in regards to the topic and issue covered. The publication is sold with the idea that the publisher is not required to render accounting, officially permitted, or otherwise, qualified services. If advice is necessary, legal or professional, a practiced individual in the profession should be ordered.

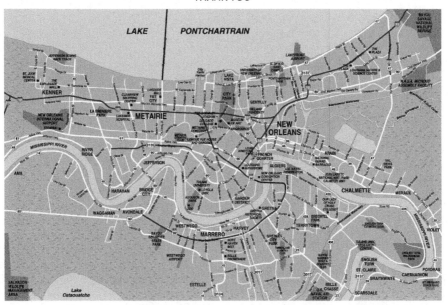